IMAGES
of Aviation

THE ORIGINAL
HELL'S ANGELS

303RD BOMBARDMENT
GROUP OF WORLD WAR II

IMAGES
of Aviation

THE ORIGINAL
HELL'S ANGELS
303RD BOMBARDMENT
GROUP OF WORLD WAR II

Valerie Smart

ARCADIA
PUBLISHING

Published by Arcadia Publishing
Charleston, South Carolina

Printed in the United States of America

Library of Congress Catalog Card Number: 2001090269

For all general information contact Arcadia Publishing at:
Telephone 843-853-2070
Fax 843-853-0044
E-mail sales@arcadiapublishing.com
For customer service and orders:
Toll-Free 1-888-313-2665

Visit us on the Internet at www.arcadiapublishing.com

To Uncle Kaz and Auntie Molly from your "Little One."
Also to the generations of families out there who have
not yet taken the time to listen to the stories of your
elders—do so now, before it is too late. There are pages
of history and many life lessons to be learned from them.

CONTENTS

ACKNOWLEDGMENTS

Special thanks to the 303rd Bombardment Group for the use of its Web site at www.303rd.com and to all of the people who help maintain this site as an invaluable resource for keeping the memory and honor of the 303rd alive.

Very special thanks to "CJ," Kim, Andi, Jen, Michael, John, Brian, Samantha, Craig, Darbe, Joey, Doc, Brett, Nathan, and my Dean for the excitement you all shared with me throughout this project.

INTRODUCTION

During World War II, there was a famed B-17 aircraft named "Hell's Angels." The men who worked together to keep the plane flying over Hitler's occupied Europe, those of the U.S. Army Air Force's 303rd Bombardment Group, were the first in the 8th Air Force to complete 25 missions from the group's base in Molesworth, England.

These men, or "Hell's Angels" as they became known, went on to complete 40 missions without ever turning back to base for mechanical failure. Because of this outstanding record, the ground crew chief, M.Sgt. Fabian S. Folmer, was awarded the Legion of Merit. The citation reads, in part, as follows:

> For exceptionally meritorious conduct in the performance of outstanding service as crew chief of a bomber aircraft from 17 October 1942, to 27 August 1943. Sergeant Folmer supervised the maintenance of an airplane, which completed thirty-nine successive combat missions over enemy territory without mechanical failure. He maintained this record in spite of technical difficulties, unfavorable and inclement weather, and with only a small ground crew. His skill, efficiency, untiring energy, and devotion to duty reflect great credit upon himself and the armed forces of the United States.

The crew indeed overcame seemingly insurmountable odds—during a mission to Veresack, Hell's Angels lost one of its engines. In order to make sure that the plane would be ready for the next mission, Folmer and the ground crew installed a new engine in 10 hours—a task that usually took 15 to 18 hours. During its year of service, they patched more than 200 holes caused by enemy fire in the plane's shell. These men went on to complete 48 missions, never having a member of the crew wounded or killed. (Although two crew members were lost when they were flying as substitute crew members in other planes).

On February 26, 1944, several members of the ground crew—M.Sgt. Fabian S. Folmer (Mansfield, Ohio), S.Sgt. Kasmer Wegrzyn (Chicopee, Massachusetts), S.Sgt. Ernest H. Touhey (Mountain Home, Arkansas), T.Sgt. Edward A. West Jr. (Newport News, Virginia), Sgt. Wilson F. Fairfield (Southbridge, Massachusetts), Sgt. John R. Kosilla (North Tarrytown, New York)—and the current pilot of the plane, Capt. John R. Johnston (Orlando, Florida), along with the original pilot of the plane, Capt. Irl E. Baldwin (Yakima, Washington), were commissioned to an "industrial morale tour" of war plants across the country. These men, who were on leave of absence, once again gathered in their famous plane and traveled from coast to coast, with stops in Paterson, New Jersey; Harrison, New Jersey; Canton, Ohio; Columbus, Ohio; Wright Field, Ohio; South Bend, Indiana; Chicago, Illinois; Cheyenne, Wyoming; Denver, Colorado; Butte, Missouri; and Los Angeles, California.

Other members of the flight crew included Capt. Harold Fulghum (Lubbock, Texas), 1st Lt. Paryley W. Madsen Jr. (Provo, Utah), 1st Lt. Donald R. Bone (Temple, Oklahoma), Sgt. James E. Rodrigues (South Ozone Park, New York), Sgt. Russell M. Warren (Sante Fe, New Mexico), Sgt. Allerton F. Medbaugh Jr. (New Milford, Connecticut), Sgt. Harry J. Brody (Glendive, Missouri), Sgt. Dennis Weiskopf (Miami, Florida), Sgt. Harold E. Godwin (Los Angeles, California), and 1st Lt. Ripley W. Joy (San Franciso, California). Each member of the crew holds the Distinguished Flying Cross and the Aid Medal.

Other members of the ground crew included Sgt. Robert C. Whitson (Achille, Oklahoma), Sgt. John J. O'Brien (Boston, Massachusetts), Sgt. George A. Roberts (Statesbury, West Virginia), Pvt. William C. Holman (Northport, Alabama), Pvt. George C. Kelly (North Hollywood, California), and Pvt. Ival E. Salisbury (Howard, Kansas).

Although the plane began its life in combat with the name "D for Dog" when it met its first crew at Kellogg Field in Michigan in 1942, it is reported that on a later flight to Berlin, the crew voted that Hell's Angels was a more fitting name for the hell the crew was experiencing in the skies and for the peace the crew was hoping to secure on Earth below. According to newspaper reports of the day, Capt. Irl E. Baldwin suggested the name Hell's Angels, after the movie of the same name, or, as one crewman said, "This is the closest to hell that angels will ever get!"

More than 50 men flew in Hell's Angels from November 17, 1942, when the plane left to begin its combat career in England, until December 13, 1943, when the plane returned to the base after its final mission. During that year, Hell's Angels dropped more than 250,000 pounds of bombs over Europe. With its second captain, Irl E. Baldwin, the plane was used as the squadron lead ship. With its next pilot, 1st Lt. William Monahan (Dorchester, Massachusetts), the plane served in a wing position.

However, the crew of Hell's Angels was only one in a squadron of hundreds of crews that performed such heroic acts during the war. The first 8th U.S. Army Air Force attack on occupied Europe took place on September 17, 1942. The 303rd Bombardment Group was constituted on January 28, 1942, and activated on February 3, 1942, at Gowan Field, Boise, Idaho. The 303rd was made up of the following squadrons: 358th, 359th, 360th, and 427th.

Despite the fact that each of the crew in the 303rd had a uniquely named and painted plane, with names like "Memphis Belle," "Knock-out Dropper," and "Vicious Virgin," on January 7, 1944, it was decided that the entire 303rd would adopt the name Hell's Angels. This was done in part for security reasons but also to honor the victorious record of the crew of the original plane Hell's Angels.

The name Hell's Angels has now come to represent the nearly 10,000 men who fought over Europe as part of the 303rd—the first heavy bomb group to complete 300 missions from an American base in England. During these 300 missions, the 303rd destroyed 372 enemy aircraft, damaged 180, and "probably" destroyed another 101. As a group, they went on to complete 364 missions and earn a deserved place in the victory of World War II.

One

THE PLANE
HELL'S ANGELS

She's done a swell job on Hitler's Fortress. She dropped more than 150,000 pounds of bombs. She left her calling card on Lorient, Rennes, Rouen, Amiens, Lille, Rotterdam, Antwerp, Vegesack, and the old girl has more than earned her keep. We believe her to be perhaps the most fought ship in the U.S. Air Force. . . . There was one time when it seemed impossible that a ship so badly crippled could have made it home. But she did. She's a ship that Hitler will never forget.

—Capt. Irl Baldwin and M.Sgt. Fabian Folmer on the plane Hell's Angels.

That ship had some luck—no matter what kind of stuff the Jerries threw up at her, she always came home with her usual report, "Bombs on target."

—M.Sgt. Fabian Folmer.

This photograph offers a rear view of the Hell's Angels B-17 aircraft as it sits idle on an

American runway.

This image offers a front view of the plane as it sits parked on a runway. Note the artwork of a cherub wearing roller skates and carrying a bomb. The artwork was originally designed and painted by Pfc. Bernard K. Kastenbaum in late 1942. It was later repainted by S.Sgt. Harold E. Godwin.

Several B-17 planes are seen here parked on a runway. The B-17, or Flying Fortress, was known as a revolutionary weapon. Its dimensions are as follows: length, 74 feet 9 inches; wingspan, 103 feet 10 inches; height, 19 feet; gross weight, about 60,000 pounds; average bomb load, 5,000 pounds; cruising speed, 211 miles per hour; horsepower, 4,800; and an armament of 12 .50-caliber machine guns.

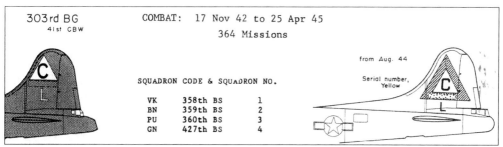

Shown is an illustration of the tail markings of the B-17s that were flown by members of the 303rd Bombardment Group, part of the 41st Combat Wing of the 8th U.S. Army Air Force, including the Hell's Angels plane. The 303rd was made up of the following squadrons: 358th, 359th, 360th, and 427th. Between November 17, 1942, and April 25, 1945, they flew a total of 364 missions. (Graphic courtesy of the New England Air Museum.)

The right side of the nose of the Hell's Angels plane was marked with two rows of small drawings of bombs—a tally of the 48 successful bombing missions the plane completed over Hitler's Europe. The plane dropped more than 250,000 pounds of bombs throughout its battle days, with the incredible record of never having a crew member in the plane injured or killed. Sgt. Kasmer Wegrzyn is shown here servicing the plane.

Here is an underside view of another B-17 that was part of the 303rd—the "Spook." This photograph shows off the plane's wingspan of nearly 104 feet.

Shown in this photograph is the front left of a B-17 plane with some of the members of the Hell's Angels crew gathered underneath. Throughout its combat career, the Hell's Angels plane went through 16 engines, 9 tires, 5 sets of brakes, 3 landing gears, and innumerable superchargers and oil-cooling systems. (Photograph courtesy of the AAF Materiel Command.)

The underbelly of Hell's Angels was covered with signatures of members of the 8th U.S. Army Air Force. The men signed the plane before it was commissioned for a war-plant tour of America in 1944. Here, three members of the ground crew are shown loading bombs into the plane.

In this view, some unidentified men gather under the wing of a B-17 plane. This perspective shows off how massive the bombers were—approximately 75 feet long and 19 feet high.

Three ground crew members of the 8th U.S. Army Air Force service a B-17 plane in this view. The ground crew members worked day and night to prepare the planes for combat missions and then to repair the planes when they returned home after the missions.

This is a view of the Hell's Angels plane in its early days, before it went to battle and accumulated more than 200 battle wounds. This photograph was taken before its crew had a chance to finish painting the nose art.

Two

THE MEN
OF HELL'S ANGELS

*For 48 missions the giant bomber's ground crew stayed at an advanced base in England
while "Hell's Angels" gallant combat crew pierced the hell of Nazi flak and fighter plane
fire to drop ton after ton of bombs on Hitler's Fortress Europa. For untold hours these men
sweated out each of the 48 missions. There were scars, yes, but the combat crew always
came back intact, thanks to the combination of aerial combat teamwork and a plane kept
in perfect fighting trim by the "invisible crew," six mechanical wizards who, sometimes,
practically overhauled the Fortress in a matter of hours between missions so that
"Hell's Angels" would be a perfect fighting machine for every mission.*

(Quotation courtesy of the AAF Materiel Command)

*Speaking of this Schweinjurt raid, on that mission, it was almost eight hours from the
time we took off to the time we landed back. We encountered practically everything we were
briefed on; in fact, we fought our way in and fought our way out. I recall looking off to my
right side after we had passed Frankfort. We were well in Germany at the time and . . . I saw
three B-17s explode in mid-air. We had a pretty good run on our target. As we made
our run, we could see the other ships dropping their bombs. It was only a matter
of minutes until that factory was in flames.*

—Capt. John R. Johnston.

This picture shows some members of the Hell's Angels crew who participated in a war-plant tour of the United States in the spring of 1944. From left to right are S.Sgt. Ernest H. Touhey,

Sgt. John R. Kosilla, S.Sgt. Kasmer Wegrzyn, T.Sgt. Edward A. West Jr., M.Sgt. Fabian S. Folmer, Sgt. Wilson F. Fairfield, Capt. Ira Baldwin, and Capt. John R. Johnston.

Posing are some of the ground crew members who helped the Hell's Angels achieve their record-breaking streak of completing 39 missions before having to turn back to base on the 40th because of mechanical failure. Shown in the pilot's cabin is Capt. John R. Johnston. The others, from left to right, are Sgt. John R. Kosilla, Sgt. Wilson F. Fairfield, S.Sgt. Kasmer Wegrzyn, S.Sgt. Ernest Touhey, S.Sgt. Edward A. West Jr., and M.Sgt. Fabian S. Folmer (crew chief).

In this view are some early members of the Hell's Angels ground crew on October 10, 1943. Identified in the front row are M.Sgt. Fabian Folmer (left) and Sgt. Ernest Toughey (center). In the back row are Sgt. Wilson Fairfield (far left), Sgt. John Kosilla (second from left), and Sgt. Kasmer Wegrzyn (center). The others are known to be Sgt. Robert Whitson, Sgt. John O'Brien, and Pvt. George Kelly.

Members of the Hell's Angels crew are seen here with the tail end of their famed plane. The ground crew was made up of Sgt. Robert C. Whitson, Sgt. John J. O'Brien, Sgt. George A. Roberts, Pvt. William C. Holman, Pvt. George C. Kelly, Pvt. Ival E. Salisbury, M.Sgt. Fabian S. Folmer, S.Sgt. Kasmer Wegrzyn, S.Sgt. Ernest H. Touhey, T.Sgt. Edward A. West Jr., Sgt. Wilson F. Fairfield, and Sgt. John R. Kosilla.

In this view, members of the Hell's Angels crew are hanging out near the wing of their plane. Although this photograph depicts a warm day, the ground crew also spent many dark, freezing nights repairing the plane by flashlight because of blackout conditions at their England base.

Seen to the right and below is S.Sgt. Kasmer
Wegrzyn of Chicopee, Massachusetts. At
19 years old, Wegrzyn was one of the youngest
members of the Hell's Angels.

These images show Capt. Irl Baldwin of Yakima, Washington. Baldwin was the original pilot of the Hell's Angels plane. Under his direction, the plane flew as squadron lead ship. Baldwin was the one who named the plane Hell's Angels.

Sgt. John R. Kosilla of North Tarrytown, New York, is seen in this view. (Photograph courtesy AAF Materiel Command.)

Sgt. Ernest Touhey of Mountain Home, Arkansas, is seen here.

Capt. John R. Johnston of Orlando,
Florida, poses in these two images.
Johnston was the last Hell's Angels pilot
to fly the plane in combat.

M.Sgt. Fabian S. Folmer of
Mansfield, Ohio, is seen here.

Seen here is T.Sgt. Edward A. West Jr. of Newport News, Virginia.

Sgt. Wilson Fairfield and an unidentified woman pose in a photograph taken on the war-plant tour in 1944. The tour gave the men a chance to be reunited with their wives and girlfriends.

Sgt. Edward A. West Jr. and an unidentified member of the 303rd catch a cigarette near a U.S. Army Air Force vehicle.

Members of the Hell's Angels are shown here during a light moment. From left to right are the following: unidentified, Sgt. Edward Touhey, Sgt. Fabian S. Folmer, Sgt. Wilson Fairfield, Sgt. Kasmer Wegrzyn, and unidentified.

Members of the Hell's Angels ground crew—Sgt. John Kosilla (far left) and three unidentified members—pose with a B-17.

Capt. Irl E. Baldwin (left) and Sgt. Kasmer Wegrzyn get a lift from a U.S. Army Air Force vehicle. Before new recruits joined life on a base, they were subject to rumors that the ground crews and the flight crews did not get along and avoided each other, but this photograph shows how wrong that assumption was.

Sgt. Kasmer Wegrzyn (left) and an unidentified member of the Hell's Angels play with a pet dog at a U.S. Army Air Force base.

U.S. Army Air Force officials gather behind members of the Hell's Angels, who are shown kneeling. The Hell's Angels are, from left to right, S.Sgt. Ernest H. Touhey, Capt. John R. Johnston, Sgt. John Kosilla, S.Sgt. Kasmer Wegrzyn, T.Sgt. Edward A. West Jr., M.Sgt. Fabian Folmer, and Sgt. Wilson F. Fairfield.

Three

LIFE IN THE U.S. ARMY AIR FORCE

The Focke-Wulfs were a couple hundred strong and they stuck with us for two hours and 20 minutes, went with us right over the target, dived among us in and out of their own flak, flew right under our wings until we could have leaned out and touched them. They were completely reckless and we shot them down like barnyard chickens. We used up 8,000 rounds of ammunition in that scrap.

—Capt. Donald R. Bone on the raid on Kiel.

I would like to tell you a little something about the ground crew here. They have been together about two years as a team, have spent about eighteen months on Hell's Angels. During that time Hell's Angels has been very fortunate. Over two hundred holes in it have been patched by Sergeant Wegrzyn and crew. It has had nineteen engine changes. It has to its credit eighteen German fighters and it went on its first forty raids without ever turning back due to a mechanical failure.

—Capt. John R. Johnston on the ground crew of Hell's Angels.

An unidentified member of the U.S. Army Air Force writes a letter during his free time.

Two unidentified ground crew members of the U.S. Army Air Force find time for a game of chess in between servicing planes.

36

Shown here are members of the ground crew of Hell's Angels. In the front row is Sgt. Fabian Folmer (left). In the back row are Sgt. Kasmer Wegrzyn (far left) and Sgt. John Kosilla (third from left). The others include Sgt. Robert Whitson, Sgt. John O' Brien, and Sgt. George A. Roberts.

The Hell's Angels ground crew strikes another pose here. In the front row are Sgt. Fabian Folmer (center) and Sgt. Kasmer Wegrzyn (far right). In the back row is Sgt. John Kosilla (center). The others include Sgt. Robert Whitson, Sgt. John O' Brien, and Pvt. George C. Kelly.

Sgt. Kasmer Wegrzyn is bundled up for the freezing temperatures that the 303rd endured throughout the winter in England.

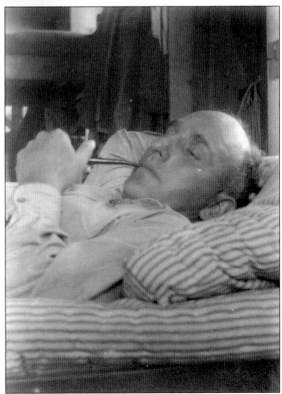

An unidentified member of the 8th U.S. Army Air Force finds time to rest and relax in his squadron's bunker.

Capt. Irl E. Baldwin (right) prepares to cross the street to enjoy an afternoon off the base.

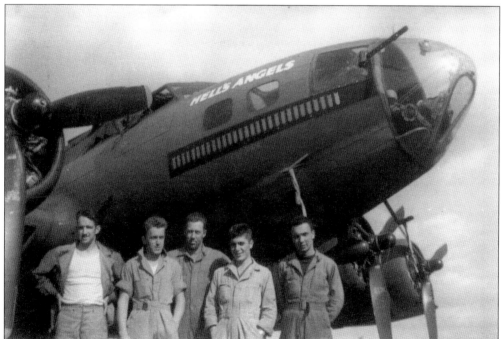

Posing with the plane that they meticulously maintained are members of the ground crew. Identified are Sgt. Wilson Fairfield (far left) and Sgt. Kasmer Wegrzyn (second from left). The others include Sgt. Robert Whitson, Sgt. John O'Brien, and Sgt. George Roberts.

GOWEN FIELD
BOISE, IDAHO

DATE February 18, 1942

SIGNATURE _Kasmer Wegrzyn_ 11008135

A.S.N.

Pfc. Kasmer Wegrzyn

NAME TYPED

HAS PERMISSION TO ENTER AND LEAVE GOWEN FIELD

Charles C. Sheridan

SIGNATURE ORGANIZATION COMMANDER

31st Reconn. Sqdn.

ORGANIZATION

THIS PERMIT WILL BE TURNED IN TO THE PROVOST MARSHAL'S OFFICE UPON TERMINATION OF DUTY AT AIR BASE.

RAY E. SWAIN
1st Lt. A.C.
Provost Marshall

Identification passes like this one were given to members of the U.S. Army Air Force who were stationed at Gowen Field (in Boise, Idaho) before heading off to the war front in Europe. The 303rd was formed while at Gowen Field.

First Reconnaissance Squadron (H) AFCC
PERMANENT PASS - Westover Field, Mass.

PASTE
PHOTO
HERE

Kasmer Wegrzyn

NAME

Pvt   11008135

RANK   A S N

Is authorized to be absent from the Air Base when not on duty.

Wm A. Matheny

WM. A. MATHENY,
Major Air Corps, Comdg.

Shown is a 1st Reconnaissance Squadron pass for Westover Field in Chicopee, Massachusetts, where some members of the 303rd, including Kasmer Wegrzyn, trained before going to Gowen Field to receive further training for the war.

40

This is the symbol identifying the 8th U.S. Army Air Force. Members of the 303rd wore the symbol as a patch on their uniform jackets.

Members of the 303rd can be seen attending early-morning Mass on February 21, 1943, at their base in Molesworth, England.

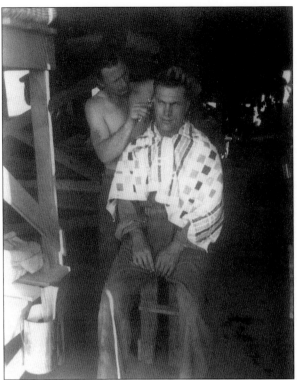

Here, a member of the 303rd is getting a buzz cut in a makeshift barbershop in the barracks.

An unidentified member of the 303rd sweeps out the barracks at the Molesworth base. Even on the war front, these men could not escape domestic duties.

An unidentified ground crew member of the U.S. Army Air Force poses near the wing of a biplane before the men were moved to the war front in Europe. This photograph was taken on May 26, 1939.

In this view, members of a 303rd ground crew get ready to "spin up" a propeller on a B-17 plane.

United States Army

Air Corps Technical School

Be it known that

Private Kasmer Wegrzyn, 11008135

36th Materiel Squadron
26th Air Base Group, GHQ AF

has satisfactorily completed the prescribed course for

Aircraft Metal Workers

as prescribed by the Air Corps Technical School and Given by

Curtiss-Wright Technical Institute, Glendale, California

In testimony whereof and by virtue of vested authority I

do confer upon him this

DIPLOMA

Given on this twenty-third day of May

in the year of our Lord one thousand nine hundred and forty-one.

Brigadier General, U.S.A.

PRESIDENT - Curtiss-Wright Technical Institute

Commandant, Air Corps Technical Schools

This diploma from the U.S. Army Air Corps Technical School signifies that Kasmer Wegrzyn successfully completed the necessary training to work on U.S. Army aircraft. Each member of the ground crew of the 303rd would have had to receive such training to work on U.S. Army Air Force planes.

An unidentified member of the U.S. Army Air Force snowshoes during a furlough day, while stationed in America.

Shown here are members of one of the flight crews of the 303rd who have recently returned from a mission. Notice the man on the far right wearing a parachute pack. Such packs were vital in case crew members needed to bail out of a failing plane during combat.

Three unidentified members of the 303rd get in some football practice while on base at Molesworth. Members of the 303rd were active in group sporting events and even had their own baseball league.

Seen here is a building on the base of the 303rd. Although the military base was anything but glamorous, the men of the 303rd found ways to enjoy their time here through sporting events, games, and forming friendships that lasted lifetimes.

Capt. Irl Baldwin (left),
Sgt. Kasmer Wegrzyn (center), and an
unidentified man smoke their cigarettes
during a break from ground crew and
combat duties at the Molesworth base.

An unidentified U.S. Army Air Force
man enjoys a snow day while stationed at
an American base. This letter sweater
shows how many of the men joined the
armed forces while teenagers.

Two unidentified members of the U.S. Army Air Force enjoy a snow day while in training in America.

An unidentified serviceman joins children in feeding the pigeons in England during the war. Notice the advertisement in the background, which states, "It helps to win the war."

Members of the U.S. Army Air Force look sharp as they pose for a group shot during their early training days in America, before going to the war front in Europe.

Sgt. Kasmer Wegrzyn shows what every serviceman or servicewoman knew during World War II—the Salvation Army Canteen was the place to be when traveling and needing a rest.

In this view, members of the Hell's Angels wait for a bus.

Two members of the 8th U.S. Army Air Force are shown hanging their laundry to dry in the summer heat. They may have been war heroes, but they were not above laundry duty.

In this view, Sgt. Fabian Folmer finds a makeshift laundry machine in a garbage pail.

English military officials and American military officials meet at the Molesworth base. The 8th U.S. Army Air Force joined the Royal Air Force of England as allies in the war and shared the base.

Four

PREPARING FOR COMBAT

The worst flak we ever encountered was in our first raid on Bremen. It stood up in front of us like a steel curtain hanging before a storm cloud of black smoke. We looked at it and wondered how anything could hope to fly through it. Not only did we fly through it but the airplane didn't even get a scratch. Shrapnel was shrieking around us like a tornado. It was some satisfaction to give Bremen a good going-over after that.

—Capt. Irl E. Baldwin.

Forts get shot down when the pilot zigs when he ought to zag.

—Capt. Irl E. Baldwin on how to get the plane safely back to base.

In these views, S.Sgt. Kasmer Wegrzyn (left), M.Sgt. Fabian Folmer (center), and Sgt. John Kosilla prepare to load Hell's Angels with oxygen tanks—a vital component for bombardment missions because of the altitude at which the planes were flown. There are many stories of 303rd members who learned a quick lesson when they did not respect the oxygen mask. If not, he was certain to be highly uncomfortable during missions that often lasted eight hours or more and certain to pass out at high altitudes without oxygen.

Sgt. Edward A. West Jr. checks the controls in the cockpit. The ground crew would give the plane a thorough going-over before declaring it ready for combat, and the flight crew would complete a thorough safety check before taking off.

S.Sgt. Kasmer Wegrzyn checks the bombardier's compartment in the nose of the plane, making sure everything is in order before the flight crew takes on another mission. (Photograph courtesy of AAF Materiel Command.)

Members of the Hell's Angels crew work on their plane. Such careful attention is what brought the men of this plane international acclaim for dedicated service and for being the first crew to complete 40 missions without turning back to base for mechanical failure. Not every crew was so lucky, however. The U.S. Army Air Force reported 1,748 personnel casualties and 210 B-17 losses as a result of the 303rd's role in the war.

In these views, Sgt. John R. Kosilla gasses up the plane. Below, he is assisted by Sgt. Wilson F. Fairfield. The close-up views of the plane show the wear and tear it encountered on its missions—testament to the luck and skill of the men who were part of the plane's crew and kept it flying through unbelievably difficult conditions. (Photographs courtesy of AAF Materiel Command.)

Ground crew members Sgt. Wilson F. Fairfield (left), S.Sgt. Edward A. West Jr. (center), and M.Sgt. Fabian S. Folmer work to remove the propeller from one of the plane's four engines to service it. (Photograph courtesy AAF Materiel Command.)

Members of the Hell's Angels prepare the plane for battle-ready status. This photograph shows the plane being gassed up and shows off the plane's impressive size in comparison to the heroes who flew and serviced it.

Members of the Hell's Angels crew give the plane a once-over before declaring it ready to fly. The men who repaired the plane after each flight knew its every nook and potential problem spots.

S.Sgt. Kasmer Wegrzyn checks one of the four engines of the plane. The mechanics who worked on the plane kept it flying for 800 hours of operational flight and 300 hours of combat flying.

Missions of the Hell's Angels

Nov. 17, 1942	St. Nazaire	May 13, 1943	Neulte Potez
Nov. 22, 1942	Lorient	May 14, 1943	Kiel
Dec. 6, 1942	Lille	May 15, 1943	Wilhelmshafen
Jan. 3, 1943	St. Nazaire	May 17, 1943	Lorient
Jan. 13, 1943	Lille	June 26, 1943	Villacoublay
Jan. 23, 1943	Lorient	July 4, 1943	St. Nazaire
Jan. 27, 1943	Wilhelmshafen	July 10, 1943	Le Mans
Feb. 4, 1943	Emden (Hamm)	July 17, 1943	Hanover
Feb. 14, 1943	Hamm	July 25, 1943	Hamburg
Feb. 16, 1943	St. Nazaire	July 26, 1943	Hamburg
Feb. 26, 1943	Wilhelmshafen	Aug. 15, 1943	Amiens – Gilsy
Feb. 27, 1943	Brest	Aug. 16, 1943	Le bourget
March 4, 1943	Rotterdam	Aug. 17, 1943	Schweinfurt
March 6, 1943	Lorient	Aug. 19, 1943	Gilze-Rijen
March 8, 1943	Rennes	Aug. 27, 1943	Watten
March 12, 1943	Rouen	Sept. 6, 1943	Stuttgart
March 13, 1943	Amiens	Sept. 13, 1943	Nantez
March 18, 1943	Vegesack	Oct. 2, 1943	Emden
March 22, 1943	Wilhelmshafen	Oct. 9, 1943	Anklam
March 28, 1943	Rouen	Oct. 10, 1943	Coesfield
March 31, 1943	Rotterdam	Nov. 3, 1943	Wilhelmshafen
April 4, 1943	Paris	Nov. 5, 1943	Gelsenkirchen
April 5, 1943	Antwerp	Nov. 26, 1943	Bremen
May 4, 1943	Antwerp	Dec. 13, 1943	Bremen (A)
May 13, 1943	Meaulte Potez		

This is a list of the dates of the missions the Hell's Angels completed.

Unidentified members of the Hell's Angels flight crew return from a flight. Missions of the 303rd were flown at an altitude well above 20,000 feet. The temperature in the plane could drop to as low as 50 degrees below zero, and the crew wore electrically heated flight suits. Combat members of the 303rd were commissioned to fly 35 missions. (Photograph courtesy U.S. Army Air Corps.)

This is a photograph of two bombs dropping from a plane over an enemy target. The original Hell's Angels dropped approximately 250,000 pounds of such bombs on their combined 48 missions. (Photograph courtesy of the U.S. Army Air Corps.)

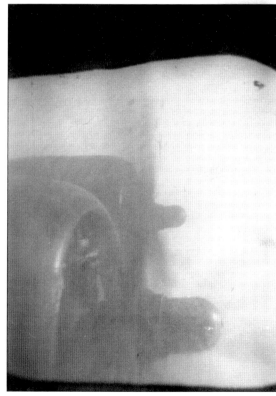

This is a photograph taken through a window in one of the B-17s, showing the engines outside.

This is a picture of six B-17s in a Flying Fortress formation. The pilots of the 303rd would practice such formations to learn the best way to defend their planes against the enemy.

This is an aerial photograph taken from one of the planes in the 303rd.

These two members of the Hell's Angels ground crew show off various views of the engines used in the B-17 they nurtured.

Sgt. Kasmer Wegrzyn is shown here in the bombardier's compartment in the plane. Notice the clips loaded into the machine gun, which was used to create flak to keep enemy planes at bay.

Five

FOR THE WAR EFFORT

*There is probably one question we have been asked more than any other: How do you
feel since you came back? I think I can speak for the rest of the boys here. Those posters may look
like a piece of paper but on those posters is what we all feel (posters on the board of
the four freedoms). When we left for overseas we might have had an automobile or any one
thing—not a big thing. Most of us took it for granted. When you get over there you think
about those things and can't have them. Then you realize what a swell place this is to live in.
We have often talked about teamwork. You think you are not doing anything. People like
you are the ones that are affording us these privileges. The people here have treated us swell,
given us what we need to fight. With good pilots like Captain Baldwin and Captain
Johnson and the swell bunch of people here, there is no reason why this country can't
come out on top. We had it and we are going to keep it.*

—M.Sgt. Fabian S. Folmer in an interview during the
Hell's Angels war-plant tour in March 1944.

The men of the 8th U.S. Army Air Force sign their names or a message to a family member in the United States before the Hell's Angels plane and a sampling of its crew leave the base in Molesworth, England, and head back home for a war-plant tour.

The crew members who were chosen to accompany the plane and represent the hundreds of crews that made up the 8th U.S. Army Air Force on a tour of aviation manufacturing plants across the United States pose in front of their heavily autographed plane. From left to right are the following: (front row) Sgt. Edward A. West Jr., Sgt. John R. Kosilla, and M.Sgt. Fabian S. Folmer; (back row) Sgt. Wilson F. Fairfield, S.Sgt. Kasmer Wegrzyn, Sgt. Edward Touhey, and Capt. John R. Johnston.

Capt. John R. Johnston shakes hands with a senior U.S. Army Air Force official before leaving England for America for the war-plant tour. Lt. Col. Ben Lyon—a member of the staff of Gen. Ira Eaker, commander of the 8th U.S. Army Air Force—was on hand for the send-off ceremony. In the background, this particular section of the plane shows how heavily autographed it was for its trip home to America.

Shown from left to right, M.Sgt. Fabian S. Folmer, Sgt. Edward A. West Jr., Sgt. Edward Touhey, and S.Sgt. Kasmer Wegrzyn simulate how happy they are to be back on American soil as the war-plant tour begins.

Capt. John R. Johnston (center) shakes hands with a senior U.S. Army Air Force official as his crew surrounds him and a crowd of well-wishers welcome the men home to America.

Members of the crew selected to participate in the war-plant tour (the first crew of the 303rd to do so during World War II) pose for a publicity photograph. From left to right are the following: (front row) Sgt. John Kosilla, Sgt. Edward A. West Jr., and Sgt. Wilson Fairfield; (back row) Capt. Irl Baldwin, Capt. John R. Johnston, and Sgt. Kasmer Wegrzyn.

At a plant of the Studebaker Company, one of the stops on the tour, Capt. John R. Johnston (left) and Sgt. Edward A. West sign autographs for the factory workers who helped manufacture the parts used in their famous airplane.

In the test-cell area of the Studebaker factory, Sgt. Edward Touhey (left) and Sgt. Kasmer Wegrzyn (on ladder) discuss the Wright Cyclone engine with Studebaker employees.

Sgt. Fabian Folmer shakes hands with a Studebaker employee as Capt. Irl Baldwin looks on. The purpose of the tour was to "raise the morale" of such workers.

The Hell's Angels enjoyed many lavish meals on their American tour as thanks for the sacrifices they made on the war front. This luncheon at the Studebaker factory is an example.

This is an example of one of the war posters displayed throughout America to rally support for the cause and to sell war bonds. This one directly promotes the U.S. Army Air Forces. (Photograph courtesy of the 303rd Bomb Group.)

This is a war poster promoting the Flying Fortress, also known as the B-17 bomber plane. (Photograph courtesy of the 303rd Bomb Group.)

This war poster features one of the planes of the mighty 303rd, which was known for its creative designs on the noses of its planes. (Photograph courtesy of the 303rd Bomb Group.)

SILENCE MEANS **SECURITY**

...we here highly resolve *that these dead shall not have died in vain* ...

REMEMBER DEC. 7th!

This poster is one of the more chilling ones, promising that the Pearl Harbor attack of December 7, 1941, will never be forgotten. (Photograph courtesy of the 303rd Bomb Group.)

Rallying support for the cause by promoting the importance of the Flying Fortresses in the war, this poster calls for Americans to honor the sacrifices being asked of them, which were testament to their patriotism. (Photograph courtesy of the 303rd Bomb Group.)

These are a few thousand of the fans who turned out to see the Hell's Angels when they visited a factory in Oklahoma City. (Photograph courtesy AAF Materiel Command.)

One of the captains of the Hell's Angels crew, Irl E. Baldwin, takes the microphone to relate tales of battle over Hitler's Europe to a crowd assembled at one of the war-plant stops in America. On the far left, notice the large crowd assembled to hear Baldwin speak.

Sgt. Kasmer Wegrzyn and an unidentified member of the Hell's Angels take the podium at the Timken Roller Bearing Company in Columbus, Ohio, on March 15, 1944, to speak to the workers there. Notice all of the women in the audience, many of whom, for the first time in their lives, went to work in the factories while their husbands and brothers were on the war front.

Members of the Hell's Angels did receive their share of attention on the war-plant tour in the spring of 1944, but it was still a treat for them to meet with some of the most popular movie stars of the day, Humphrey Bogart and Lauren Bacall.

Perhaps some would describe these men as the luckiest of the Hell's Angels, as they got to pose with some of the most popular entertainers of the 1940s. From left to right are the following: (front row) Hoagy Carmichael, Capt. Irl E. Baldwin, Humphrey Bogart, S.Sgt. Ernest Touhey, Lauren Bacall, and Sgt. Wilson Fairfield; (back row) M.Sgt. Fabian Folmer, Sgt. Edward A. West Jr., Capt. John R. Johnston, Sgt. John Kosilla, Walter Brennen, and Sgt. Kasmer Wegrzyn.

One lucky lady gets a boost from the Hell's Angels as she takes a closer look at the writing on the plane, when it stopped at the Boeing Aircraft Company in Seattle, Washington. This photograph shows off the number of bombing raids the crew participated in, as they kept a tally—drawing one bomb for each time the plane returned from a successful mission (a total of 48).

Sgt. Wilson F. Fairfield (left) and Sgt. John R. Kosilla sign autographs for some of their admirers at the Studebaker factory. Although these women were admirers of the Hell's Angels, they were also the ones who helped manufacture the parts that kept their plane and many others flying during the war.

Sgt. Kasmer Wegrzyn (center) gets the royal treatment and a banana split from two unidentified plant managers at one of the crew's stops on the tour.

The crew is dressed to the nines for its visit to the Studebaker Flying Fortress Engine Plant in South Bend, Indiana, on March 18, 1944. From left to right are Sgt. Fabian Folmer, Capt. Irl E. Baldwin, Sgt. Ernest Touhey, Sgt. Kasmer Wegrzyn, Capt. John R. Johnston, Sgt. Edward A. West Jr., Sgt. John Kosilla, and Sgt. Wilson Fairfield.

When the crew visited the various plants around the country, they received special day passes to roam around the factories, such as this card, which was granted to Sgt. Kasmer Wegrzyn when the crew visited the Studebaker factory and which was hand-signed by the president and vice president of the company.

In this view, an unidentified woman who worked at the Boeing Aircraft Company in Seattle, Washington, signs her name to the underbelly of the Hell's Angels plane as she is given a boost by Sgt. Edward A. West Jr. (left) and Sgt. Kasmer Wegrzyn (right) as Sgt. Ernest Touhey and Sgt. Wilson Fairfield (far right) look on.

Members of the Hell's Angels meet with more famous folks of the day. From left to right are the following: (front row) Capt. Irl E. Baldwin, unidentified, actor Paul Hendried, and actor Peter Lorre; (back row) Sgt. Ernest Touhey, Sgt. Edward West Jr., Capt. John R. Johnston, actress Hedy Lamarr, Sgt. Wilson Fairfield, Sgt. John R. Kosilla, unidentified, Sgt. Fabian S. Folmer, and Sgt. Kasmer Wegrzyn.

The Hell's Angels joined the employees of the Curtiss Wright Technical Institute Plating Laboratory in their work overalls during their stop there.

The Hell's Angels brush shoulders with another star of the day—columnist Hedda Harper.

During the tour, the Hell's Angels also had some down time, including time to pose for this fun photograph. From left to right are Sgt. Kasmer Wegrzyn, Sgt. Edward West Jr., Sgt. Fabian Folmer, and Sgt. Wilson Fairfield.

In this view, Sgt. Ernest Touhey practices his swing during some free time on the war-plant tour.

In this view, the Hell's Angels are enjoying an afternoon off from their touring duties. From left to right are the following: (front row) Sgt. Kasmer Wegrzyn, unidentified, Sgt. Wilson Fairfield, and unidentified; (back row) Sgt. Fabian Folmer.

Members of the Hell's Angels could even count on having their picture snapped while waiting for hotel room keys. From left to right are Sgt. Kasmer Wegrzyn, Sgt. Fabian Folmer, Sgt. Wilson Fairfield, Capt. John R. Johnston, Sgt. Edward West Jr., an unidentified woman, Sgt. John R. Kosilla, and Sgt. Ernest Touhey.

This is an example of how the Hell's Angels captivated the country during their trip across America—a page from the *South Bend Tribune* of South Bend, Indiana, when the crew visited that city during the week of March 12–20, 1944.

In this photograph, Sgt. John Kosilla simulates how happy he is to be home.

Crew members pose for one last shot before the tour is over. From left to right are Capt. Irl E. Baldwin, Sgt. Fabian S. Folmer, Sgt. Edward West Jr., Capt. John R. Johnston, Sgt. Kasmer Wegrzyn, Sgt. Ernest Touhey, Sgt. Wilson Fairfield, and Sgt. John R. Kosilla.

Capt. John Johnston greets a senior member of one of the war plants they visited on the tour while the rest of the crew looks on.

This is one of the small airfields that the Hell's Angels landed their plane at during the tour. This is the Grand Central Air Terminal in the western United States.

Shown above and below, members of the Hell's Angels enjoy a day at the beach as a small vacation during the tour.

Sgt. Fabian Folmer is "on edge" during some free time on the war-bond tour. Being on edge this time, however, was quite different from the days he would be on edge waiting for the Hell's Angels plane to return to base after a mission.

Capt. John Johnston takes time to enjoy the scenery while on the war-plant tour—something he did not have much time for when he was busy completing his required 35 missions as a member of the 8th U.S. Army Air Force.

Sgt. Ernest Touhey takes on a safari look while touring the western United States during the war-plant morale tour.

Sgt. Kasmer Wegrzyn goes from working on planes to rowing a boat during some well-deserved time off back home in America during the war-plant tour.

Shown above and below, unidentified actors and actresses pose near a plane named "Hell Hoppin." There is no record of a B-17 by that name in the 303rd. These people probably joined together while filming a movie about the war or for a promotional event to sell war bonds.

M.Sgt. Fabian Folmer (front left) and Capt. John R. Johnston "review" some procedural information for the plane during this press photograph to publicize the war-plant tour while Edward West Jr. and an unidentified member of the crew load the plane.

INSTRUCTIONS

1 This book is valuable. Do not lose it.

2 Each stamp authorizes you to purchase rationed goods in the quantities and at the times designated by the Office of Price Administration. Without the stamps you will be unable to purchase those goods.

3 Detailed instructions concerning the use of the book and the stamps will be issued. Watch for those instructions so that you will know how to use your book and stamps. Your Local War Price and Rationing Board can give you full information.

4 Do not throw this book away when all of the stamps have been used, or when the time for their use has expired. You may be required to present this book when you apply for subsequent books.

Rationing is a vital part of your country's war effort. Any attempt to violate the rules is an effort to deny someone his share and will create hardship and help the enemy.

This book is your Government's assurance of your right to buy your fair share of certain goods made scarce by war. Price ceilings have also been established for your protection. Dealers must post these prices conspicuously. Don't pay more.

Give your whole support to rationing and thereby conserve our vital goods. Be guided by the rule:

"If you don't need it, DON'T BUY IT."

16—32299-1 ☆ U. S. GOVERNMENT PRINTING OFFICE : 1942

This is a ration stamp book used by civilians during World War II to limit the amount of consumer goods that could be purchased by each family during the war. Inside would be small

UNITED STATES OF AMERICA
OFFICE OF PRICE ADMINISTRATION

CT 67 885

WAR RATION BOOK No. 3

Void if altered

Identification of person to whom issued: PRINT IN FULL

GENE   M.   BRYANT

(First name)   (Middle name)   (Last name)

Street number or rural route 1630 Lyman Pl. N.E.

City or post office Wash.   State D.C.

AGE	SEX	WEIGHT	HEIGHT	OCCUPATION
27	Female	135 Lbs.	5 Ft. 6 In.	House Wife

SIGNATURE Gene M Bryant

(Person to whom book is issued. If such person is unable to sign because of age or incapacity, another may sign in his behalf

WARNING

This book is the property of the United States Government. It is unlawful to sell it to any other person, or to use it or permit anyone else to use it, except to obtain rationed goods in accordance with regulations of the Office of Price Administration. Any person who finds a lost War Ration Book must return it to the War Price and Rationing Board which issued it. Persons who violate rationing regulations are subject to $10,000 fine or imprisonment, or both.

OPA Form No. R-130

LOCAL BOARD ACTION

Issued by _____
(Local board number)   (Date)

Street address _____

City _____   State _____

(Signature of issuing officer)

blue stamps that were used when making purchases. The back of the book reads, "If you don't need it, don't buy it."

By the time it finished its trip across America, the Hell's Angels plane was covered from nose to tail and wing to wing in signatures and messages of not only the men of the 303rd but also of their fans in America. Sgt. John Kosilla is shown here with the plane.

Six

OTHER CREWS
IN THE 303RD

I will never forget when the ships come back from the raids. They come over the field
circling and some of them drop red flares. They aren't doing that just for fun.
Those red flares mean that there are dead or wounded on the ship. All
attention is given to that ship. The crews all rush out to give blood or do whatever is
necessary. Those ships have the priority of landing. The planes circle the field until those
ships have been taken care of. Then the ground crews go back to their own ships. There
is a loud speaker system at the headquarters that reaches every building. The plane
gives the information to the hospital as to what type of blood is needed and all the boys
get out their dog tags to see what type of blood he has. If they have that type they just
take off for the hospital right away. Our barracks were about half a mile from the hospital
and by the time we got away you couldn't get within 500 yards of the hospital.

—Sgt. Edward A. West Jr., on how all of the
crew of the 303rd worked together.

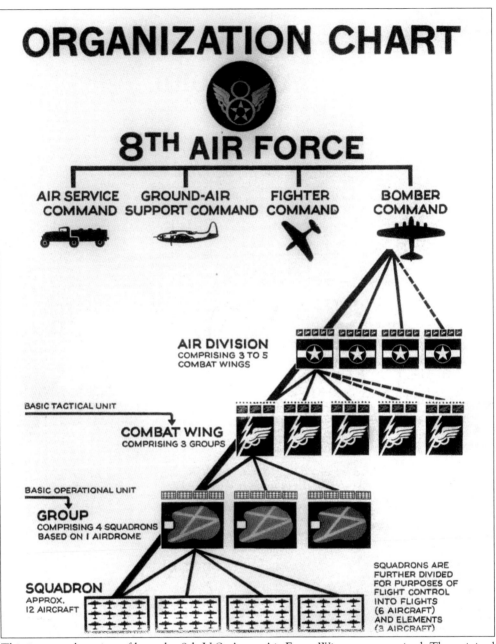

This is an explanation of how the 8th U.S. Army Air Force Wing was organized. The original Hell's Angels were part of the 358th Bombardment Squadron of the 303rd Bombardment Group. Other squadrons in the 303rd were the 359th, 360th, and 427th. (Photograph courtesy Army Air Forces Aid Society.)

These are unidentified members of one of the crews that flew the B-17 "Yankee Doodle."

Shown here are members of the Loren W. Bohle crew of the 358th Bombardment Squadron. From left to right are the following: (front row) S.Sgt. Jack C. Smith, Sgt. Norman Genter, S.Sgt George C. Aldous, T.Sgt Wayne C. Sproule, and Sgt. Robert F. Bigelow; (back row) 1st Lt. Loren W. Bohle, Lt. Jonathan S. Swift, F/O Eugene M. "Bud" Gerhardstein, and 1st Lt. Joseph Gordon. This photograph was taken in February 1945, shortly after the crew was assigned to the 358th on February 15, 1945. (Photograph courtesy of the 303rd Bomb Group.)

Shown here are members of the Richard H. Gmernicki crew of the 358th Bombardment Squadron. From left to right are the following: (front row) 2nd Lt. Richard H. Gmernicki, 2nd Lt. Chester G. Judd, F/O Joseph C. Guerrieri, and 2nd Lt. William M. Jones; (back row) T.Sgt. Elwood A. Griffith, Cpl. Ray R. Cooper, T.Sgt. Raymond N. Calenberg, Cpl. Bernard Greenberg, Cpl. John W. McClymont, and S.Sgt. Thomas A. Henn. This crew was assigned on September 28, 1944. (Photograph courtesy of the 303rd Bomb Group.)

Shown here are members of the Carl Morales crew of the 358th Bombardment Squadron who flew the B-17F "Sky Wolf." They are identified as 2nd Lt. Carl H. Morales, 2nd Lt. Calvin A. Swaffer, 2nd Lt. William C. Hunter, 2nd Lt. Frank E. Zasadil, T.Sgt. Francis G. Hinds, Sgt. Albert V. Carroll, Sgt. Francis J. Burns, Sgt. John E. Hill, Sgt. Robert C. Blake, and S.Sgt. Van R. White.

Shown here are the following members of the William J. Monahan crew of the 358th Bombardment Squadron who flew with the B-17F Hell's Angels: (front row) 1st Lt. William J. Monahan, Lt. Martin L. "Pete" Clark, 2nd Lt. William P. Maher, and 2nd Lt. Walter Hargrove; (back row) T.Sgt. M.D. Ignaczewski, S.Sgt. Frank Kimotek, S.Sgt. Walter Gasser, S.Sgt. Alfred R. Buinicky, S.Sgt. James H. Comer Jr., and S.Sgt. David Miller. This crew flew five missions with Lt. Ripley W. Joy and six missions with Lt. William J. Monahan from July 4, 1943, to August 27, 1943. This photograph was taken August 10, 1943. (Photograph courtesy of the 303rd Bomb Group.)

Shown are the following members of the Arnold S. Litman crew of the 358th Bombardment Squadron: T.Sgt. George A. Smith, T.Sgt. Francis R. Ebbighausen, S.Sgt. Paul M. Gibbs, Serax, S.Sgt. Victor H. Miller, S.Sgt. Tracy W. Lawson, S.Sgt. Buenaventur L. Castillo, Capt. Arnold S. Litman, 1st Lt. Quentin J. Gorman, Capt. Lawrence C. Merthan, and 1st Lt. Albert W. Stravinsky. This crew was assigned on February 4, 1944, and the photograph was taken on February 6, 1944. (Photograph courtesy of the 303rd Bomb Group.)

Shown here are the following members of the Ray W. Jess crew of the 358th Bombardment Squadron: (front row) 2nd Lt. Charles M. Box, 2nd Lt. Robert P. Davidson, 2nd Lt. Harold W. Gunn, and 1st Lt. Ray W. Jess; (back row) T.Sgt. Joseph J. Godzinski, S.Sgt. Byron W. Johnson, T.Sgt. Harold E. Smith, S.Sgt. Charles F. Hardacre, and S.Sgt. Frank M. White. (Photograph courtesy of the 303rd Bomb Group.)

Shown in this view are the following members of the Marvin H. Heckendorf crew of the 358th Bombardment Squadron: (front row) Cpl. Robert L. Barris, Cpl. Hubert W. Gallman, Cpl. Bill Windle, Cpl. Raymond W. Lary, and Cpl. David M. Koener; (back row) 2nd Lt. Marvin H. Heckendorf, 2nd Lt. Robert L. Erickson, 2nd Lt. Kenneth R. Carnahan, and Cpl. Robert J. Weaver. This crew was assigned on October 4, 1944, and this photograph was taken on December 1, 1944. (Photograph courtesy of the 303rd Bomb Group.)

Shown here are the following members of the Ernest A. Bailey Jr. crew of the 358th Bombardment Squadron: Sgt. Austin D. Deaver, Sgt. Richard P. Beamer, Sgt. Alexander F. Masson, Sgt. Gerald L. Bacon, Sgt. Frank L. Farmer, 2nd Lt. Ernest A. Bailey, 2nd Lt. Lawrence L. Fries Jr., and Lt. Fred D. Domblasser Jr. This crew was assigned on April 1, 1945, and this photograph was taken on April 3, 1945. (Photograph courtesy of the 303rd Bomb Group.)

Shown here are unidentified members of one of the crews that flew the "Eight Ball" plane. The "Eight Ball" is known as the plane that brought her crew more decorations than any other crew, including several silver stars, many Distinguished Flying Crosses, many Air Medals, and five Purple Hearts. It is also known as the plane that included actor Clark Gable among its crew when he served during World War II. This photograph was taken on May 4, 1943.

Shown here are the following members of the Ernest C. Price crew of the 358th Bombardment Squadron: (front row) Sgt. Paul R. Bilchak, Sgt. William E. Noel, Sgt. Michael T. Postek, Sgt. Keith E. Day, Sgt. John F. Reed, and Sgt. Raymond L. Cole; (back row) 1st Lt. Ernest C. Price, 1st Lt. Frederick C. Hower, 2nd Lt. Leonard S. Patillo, and 2nd Lt. Fred B. Creel. This crew was assigned on September 23, 1944. (Photograph courtesy of 303rd Bomb Group.)

Shown in this view are some unidentified members of the crew that flew the "Sky Wolf" plane. The crew is credited for taking out 20 German fighters before going down on a mission to Oschersleben. This photograph was taken on February 27, 1943.

Shown here are the following members of the Claude W. Campbell crew of the 359th Bombardment Squadron: (front row) Howard E. Hernan, Benton F. Wilson, George D. Quick, Harold A. Kraft, and Kurt W. Bachert; (back row) Claude W. Campbell, Arthur W. Miller, George M. Ririe, and Winston E. Boutelle. This crew was assigned on April 8, 1943, and this photograph was taken on July 17, 1943. (Photograph courtesy of the 303rd Bomb Group.)

Shown here are the following members of the Joe B. Arwood crew of the 360th Bombardment Squadron: (front row) Sgt. Paul A. Curry, Sgt. Thomas B. Power, Sgt. Crispen E. Sanchez, and Sgt. James B. Linn; (back row) 2nd Lt. Joe B. Arwood, 2nd Lt. Walter N. Johnson, 2nd Lt. William C. Fowler, and 2nd Lt. Clarence L. Counsell. This crew was assigned on October 2, 1944, and this photograph was taken on October 15, 1944. Two other crew members are missing from this photograph, Cpl. Leland P. Peebler and Cpl. David A. Costa, who bailed out of their plane over Presque Isle, Maine, on their way over to England and drowned. The other enlisted men also bailed out but survived. (Photograph courtesy of the 303rd Bomb Group.)

Shown here are the following members of the Robert G. App crew of the 360th Bombardment Squadron: (front row) T.Sgt. Norman L. Leach, S.Sgt. Austin M. Matlock, Sgt. Duane L. Polaski, Sgt. Joseph P. Hulterstrum, Sgt. Gene F. Brady, and Sgt. Herschell F. Nabors; (back row) 2nd Lt. Robert G. App, 2nd Lt. William S. Moody, 2nd Lt. Walter F. Dennis, and F/O Martin R. Dee. All crewmen completed their tours of 35 missions. This crew was assigned on October 4, 1944, and the photograph was taken in August 1944. (Photograph courtesy of the 303rd Bomb Group.)

Shown here are the following members of the Murdock B. McMillan Jr. crew of the 360th Bombardment Squadron: (front row) S.Sgt. Camil Debannes, Sgt. Allen H. Herr, S.Sgt. James D. Cox, Sgt. Harold Karp, and Sgt. Paul J. Noller; (back row) 1st Lt. Marvin E. Shaw, 1st Lt. Stanley Polezoes, 1st Lt. Murdock B. McMillan Jr., 1st Lt. James R. Prince, and Sgt. Leroy H. Cain. This crew was assigned on April 21, 1944, and this photograph was taken on May 17, 1944. (Photograph courtesy of the 303rd Bomb Group.)

Shown are the members of the Leonard E. Jokerst crew of the 360th Bombardment Squadron who flew the B-17F "Shangri-La." They are identified as 1st Lt. Leonard E. Jokerst, 2nd Lt. Willard H. Bergeron, 2nd Lt. Robert N. DeFeis, unidentified, T.Sgt. Alphonse B. Serwa, T.Sgt. Leroy Cline, S.Sgt. Norman A. Hemmings, S.Sgt. William H. Stephens, S.Sgt. George W. Wilson, and S.Sgt. Vernon R. Appleton. This crew was assigned on July 25, 1943, and this photograph was taken on August 12, 1943. (Photograph courtesy of the 303rd Bomb Group.)

Shown here are the following members of the Loyd D. Griffin crew of the 360th Bombardment Squadron: (front row) Loyd D. Griffin, Walter C. "Walt" Swanson, Robert L. "Bob" Taylor, and William M. "Bill" Preston; (back row) Lynwood D. "Lindy" Wiegand, William M. "Bill" Eason, Samuel L. "Sam" Edwards, Vernon E. "Gene" Schwartz, and Louis W. "Louie" Rheaume. This crew was assigned on February 9, 1943, and this photograph was taken in October 1942, in Topeka, Kansas. (Photograph courtesy of the 303rd Bomb Group.)

Members of the Max A. Christian crew of the 360th Bombardment Squadron included the following (not all names are represented in the photograph): 1st Lt. Max A. Christian, 1st Lt. John R. Francis, 1st Lt. Nyle E. Cotner, 1st Lt. Rufe H. Parrilla, T.Sgt. Carl L. Asplund, T.Sgt. Arthur P. Tibbetts, S.Sgt. James W. Hughes, Sgt. Ernest P. Lobenherz, Sgt. Hans Howald, and S.Sgt. Kenneth L. Elmore. (Photograph courtesy of the 303rd Bomb Group.)

Shown are the members of the Donald E. Stockton crew of the 427th Bombardment Squadron who flew the B-17F "Joe Btfsplk II." They are as follows: (front row) M.Sgt. Henry C. Parker, S.Sgt. Roy Q. Smith, Sgt. Carson Bryant, S.Sgt. Lee H. Amos, Sgt. Dean M. Packer, and Sgt. Marines H. Meyers; (back row) 1st Lt. Donald E. Stockton, 2nd Lt. Fort W. Lipe, 2nd Lt. Lawrence H. Grant, 2nd Lt. Lloyd A. Shirley, and 1st Lt. Quentin W. Hargrove. This crew was assigned to the 427th on May 1, 1942. (Photograph courtesy of the 303rd Bomb Group.)

Shown here are the following members of the John A. Newton crew of the 427th Bombardment Squadron who flew the B-17G "Miss Lace:" (front row) 2nd Lt. William F. Drew, 2nd Lt. Frank G. Mowatt, 1st Lt. John A. Newton, and 1st Lt. George L. Lenge; (back row) S.Sgt. John F. Hobgood, S.Sgt. James E. Reeves, S.Sgt. Albert W. Bricker, T.Sgt. James A. O'Leary, and T.Sgt. Leonard A. Turner. This crew was assigned on June 17, 1944, and this photograph was taken in June 1944. (Photograph courtesy of the 303rd Bomb Group.)

Shown here are the following members of the Philip D. Eisenwinter crew of the 427th Bombardment Squadron: (front row) 2nd Lt. Philip D. Eisenwinter, 2nd Lt. Richard C. Waggoner, 2nd Lt. Frederick J. Norman, and 2nd Lt. Robert C. Campbell; (back row) Cpl. Vester W. Warner, Sgt. William A. Murphy, Sgt. Edward E. Ross, Sgt. Paul Veljkov, and Sgt. Howard A. Grossman. Sgt. Thomas Merrill is missing from the photograph. This photograph was taken in the United States in June 1944. (Photograph courtesy of the 303rd Bomb Group.)

In these photographs, unidentified members of the 303rd Bombardment Group hang out at their base in Molesworth, England.

Seven

OTHER PLANES IN THE 303RD

Yeah, if a ship gets hurt bad enough to go into hangar and becomes a hangar queen,
Heaven help her. The other crews are pickin' on her like ants on a dead rat. Steal this
and steal that. They keep sayin, "She's a cripple and we gotta keep our ship flyin."

—S.Sgt. Kasmer Wegrzyn in an April 13, 1944
Saturday Evening Post radio dramatization.

Almost unknown is the fact that the epic change of the airplane from a biplane hung
together with struts and wires—the flying machine of World War I—to an internally braced
monoplane of extreme symmetry and power, was brought about by engineers of the Materiel
Command. So was the change from wood and fabric to all-metal construction. Manufacturers'
engineers also contributed to these Army Air Force developments. The Materiel Command,
with the aid of the American rubber industry, developed a self-sealing tank so
successful that the Germans have literally copied it, abandoning their own designs.

—From a press release from the Public Relations Section
of the AAF Materiel Command.

Shown in this view is nose art from the plane "Yardbird II," a B-17F of the 360th Bombardment Squadron. This design features a bomb-carrying man who says, "Time's a wastin." As with most of the planes in the 303rd, the men kept track of their mission with drawings of bombs on the nose of the plane. At the time of this photograph, for example, the crew has recorded 25 missions. The crew was assigned to the plane on January 29, 1943, and was reported as missing in action on October 2, 1943. The crew completed 43 missions with the plane.

Shown in this view is nose art from the "Duchess," the B-17F also known as "Sure Stuff." The crew of this plane was assigned in October 1942 and completed 59 missions before the plane returned to America on July 7, 1944.

Shown here is nose art from the B-17G "Butch," also known as "Toots." The crew of this plane was assigned on April 6, 1943, and completed 17 missions before the plane was reported as missing in action on July 25, 1943.

Shown in this view is nose art from an unidentified plane from the 303rd.

Shown here is nose art of the B-17F "Qui-9 the Bitter Dose," or the "Nasty Nine." The crew was assigned to this plane on April 8, 1943, and completed six missions before the plane was destroyed in a crash on June 25, 1943.

Nose art of the "Wallaroo," a B-17F of the 359th Bombardment Squadron, is seen in this view. The crew of this plane was assigned on April 9, 1943, and completed 35 missions before being classified as missing in action on January 14, 1944.

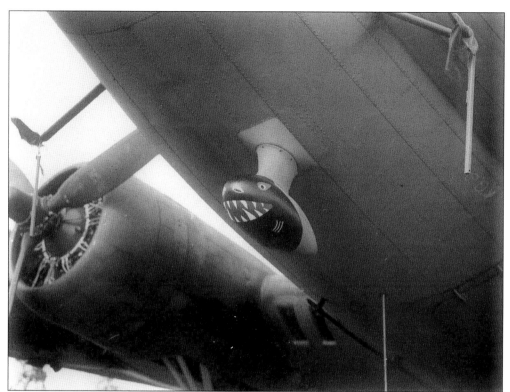

As shown in these images, members of the 303rd took any opportunity to paint humor or symbolism on their B-17s.

Shown here is a montage of some of the nose art of the planes in the 303rd. (Photograph courtesy of the Army Air Forces Aid Society.)

This photograph shows even more of the creative nose art of the planes of the 303rd, proving that the men of the 303rd were not only brave servicemen but also skilled artists. (Photograph courtesy of the Army Air Forces Aid Society.)

Although each of the planes in the 303rd was uniquely decorated with specific nose art, none was as embellished as Hell's Angels, which was marked with the words of hundreds of people. This picture, which includes the signatures of seven of the Hell's Angels on the top left, shows how many people wanted to make their mark on the plane. The signatures of the Hell's Angels are those of Capt. Irl E. Baldwin, M.Sgt. Fabian S. Folmer, S.Sgt. Kasmer Wegrzyn, S.Sgt. Ernest Touhey, Sgt. John Kosilla, T.Sgt. Edward A. West Jr., and Sgt. Wilson Fairfield.

Eight

TO HONOR
AND REMEMBER

The United States Army Air Force is making history and its own traditions in this global war. It is an aerial force made up of men from all walks of life; boys just out of their teen-age whose only thought should be to become men and settle down and enjoy the community spirit and freedom of our great nation, men with wives, and children who had already taken their place in our way of life. They were students, executives, laborers, men with professional backgrounds, and others who have all joined in a common cause . . . Men who are not killers or haters, but who realize that this war is a question of the survival of the fittest; that is a serious business in which they, as Americans, have their very existence as a nation at stake and are willing to sacrifice their lives to see that our great nation will forever have those liberties and equalities that have made it a great nation. . . . There is no thought of defeat, and though they have seen their best friends and companions blown out of the skies in front of their very eyes, they have never turned back in the face of the enemy.

—From the foreword of *The First 300 Might in Flight Hell's Angels.*

The memorial honoring the 303rd Bombardment Group at the site of their former base in Molesworth, England, can be seen in this view. (Photograph courtesy of the 303rd Bomb Group.)

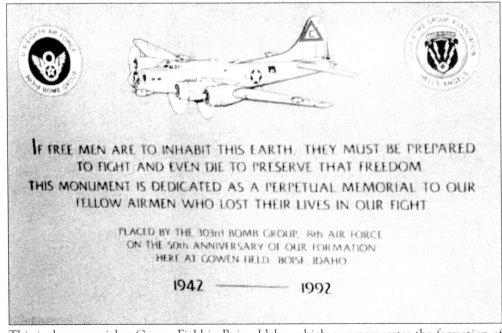

This is the memorial at Gowen Field in Boise, Idaho, which commemorates the formation of the 303rd Bombardment Group in 1942 at the field. (Photograph courtesy of the 303rd Bomb Group.)

Pilots of the 358th BS

- Arundale, Karl B.
- Bailey, Ernest A. Jr.
- Baker, John H.
- Baldwin, Irl E.
- Bailie, Homer P.
- Bass, Julius E.
- Benepe, Louis M.
- Bohle, Loren W.
- Boyce, Marvin S.
- Burton, Richard B.
- Campbell, Paul W.
- Clark, Elmo E.
- Clark, Martin L. "Pete"
- Clark, James B.
- Cunningham, Neil E.
- DaShiell, William C.
- Davis, William C.
- DeCamp, Donald F.
- Dunnica, Lawrence G.
- Elder, Damon C.
- Elliott, Albert H.
- Ferguson, Wendell Z.
- Fort, William C. Jr.
- Freeland, Troit D.
- Freeman, Clyde L.
- Frost, William N.
- Gamble, Donald
- Glass, Leroy E.
- Gmernicki, Richard H.
- Gobrecht, Harry D.
- Goering, Werner
- Goodberlet, Clarence J.
- Gordon, Joseph
- Gorman, Quentin J.
- Goss, Arthur L.
- Greenbaum, Richard D.
- Greene, Robert E.
- Griffith, Rudolph L., Jr.
- Grisham, Rufus W., Jr.
- Haas, Joseph E.
- Heckendorf, Marvin H.
- Heleen, Carl M.
- Henderson, John F.
- Hendry, John W.
- Hoffman, Raymond
- Holm, Maurice M.
- Hungerford, Merle R.
- Jameson, Chet H., Jr.
- Jess, Ray W.
- Johnson, Harlan J.
- Johnson, Hugh B.
- Johnston, John R.
- Joy, Ripley W.
- Kentsbeer, William F.
- Kyse, Walter A.
- Lake, Lester A. Jr.
- Larson, Roy A.
- Latshaw, William F.
- Leach, Joseph V.
- Lee, Gareth H.
- Lemmon, John V.
- Litman, Arnold S.
- Lord, Truman R.
- Mayer, Walter J.
- McClure, Thomas R.
- McCutcheon, George E.
- McDonald, James M.
- McKinley, Ralph C.
- McLeod, William S., Jr.
- McNamara, James F.
- Miller, Cecil W.
- Milman, Jerome
- Monahan, William J.
- Morales, Carl H.
- Moreau, Joseph A.
- Morningstar, Thomas H.
- Murray, Robert I.
- Nester, Harry E.
- Nolan, Robert J.
- O'Connor, Oran T.
- O'Connor, Robert S.
- Oxrider, George J.
- Packard, Peter L.M.
- Paullin, James R.
- Perkins, Morton C.
- Poole, Lawrence E.
- Price, Ernest C.
- Rogan, Dave L.
- Rosser, Samuel E.
- Sanders, Roy C.
- Shebeck, Daniel A.
- Smith, Alfred I.
- Smithy, Samuel C.
- Snider, Harley D.
- Snyder, Robert W.
- Stein, Lawrence J.
- Sumarlidason, Arni L.
- Swaffer, Calvin A.
- Taub, Francis R.
- Taylor, James B.
- Thompson, Frank H.
- Timken, Jack C.
- Twomey, John M.
- Vermeer, Bernard E.
- Viets, John B.
- Walker, Barton F. Jr.
- Walter, Donald R.
- Watson, Jack W.
- Watson, John P.
- Way, Henry G.
- Wise, Calder L.
- Woodard, John M.
- Woodson, William H.
- Worthley, Joe R.

This is a list of the original pilots of the 358th Bombardment Squadron. (List courtesy of the 303rd Bomb Group.)

Pilots of the 359th BS

- Akers, Robert O.
- Arnold, William J.
- Assenheimer, Edwin H.
- Bailey, Jack W.
- Bales, Ross C.
- Baltes, George E.
- Bashor, Oliver Lee
- Beasley, William M.
- Bixby, Kenneth E.
- Brabant, Patrick H.
- Brown, Malcolm E.
- Calhoun, William R.
- Call, Fred E.
- Campbell, Claude W.
- Carney, Walter J.
- Chance, Arthur F.
- Cline, William J.
- Crozier, Harry J.
- Daub, LeRoy E.
- Daum, Maurice C.
- Davis, Jack T.
- Edwards, Kenneth C.
- Eich, Henry J. Jr.
- Eldridge, Truman K.
- Embrey, Henry C.
- Eyster, Ercil F.
- Fackler, David E.
- Frazier, Eugene C.
- Goolsby, Billy M.
- Gould, Graham C.
- Grant, Ambrose G.

- Halpin, Robert H. Jr.
- Hanselman, Charles F.
- Harding, Lawrence T.
- Harrison, Weldon O.
- Henning, Clyde H.
- Hillary, Jack R.
- Hybert, Arthur J.
- Jenkins, Harry F.
- Johnson, Hans C.
- Knudson, Darwin D.
- Konsmo, George E.
- Langford, Allen W.
- Lorentz, Arthur D.
- Loughnan, Victor J.
- Lowry, William J.
- Lutz, John R.
- Mainwaring, Charles O.
- Manning, John C.
- Marsh, Richard K.
- Mattison, Robert L.
- Mauger, Warren E.
- McClung, Guy H.
- Meier, Russell W.
- Mickle, James D.
- Miller, William F.
- Moncur, Vern L.
- Moore, Thomas L.
- Moreman, Robert
- Morgan, William D.
- Moser, Clinton A.
- Nix, James S.

- O'Donnell, Thomas M.
- Pentz, Arthur H.
- Proffitt, John S. Jr.
- Purcell, William A.
- Quinn, Thomas J.
- Reddig, Arthur E.
- Reeder, D.M.
- Richeson, Marvin G.
- Rogers, Clem W.
- Roller, Jack
- Roth, Ernest L.
- Rowan, Frederick L.
- Rybaltowski, Vincent
- Sanderson, Ellis J.
- Saunders, Frank A.
- Savage, John J.
- Shoup, Noel E.
- Sirany, George R.
- Smith, Sanford T.
- Stauffer, Robert N.
- Stewart, Frederick A.
- Stoulil, Donald W.
- Stouse, Harold L.
- Tarvid, Arthur J.
- Thompson, Lawrence C.
- Tilsen, Cyril
- Towne, Harvey E.
- Underdown, Sidney L.
- Van Weelden, Douglas
- Virag, Andy R.
- Walker, Lewis M.
- Young, Elmer W.

This is a list of the original pilots of the 359th Bombardment Squadron. (List courtesy of the 303rd Bomb Group.)

Pilots of the 360th BS

- Adams, Arthur I.
- App, Robert G.
- Armfield, John M.
- Arwood, Joe B.
- Austin, Charles A.
- Baker, William T.
- Bartholomew, Dale E.
- Bennett, Paul K.
- Bentley, Andrew K.
- Bentzlin, Bartil V.
- Bergeron, Willard H.
- Bordelon, Berton A.
- Breed, William H.
- Brinkley, Pharis C.
- Brown, Leonard M.
- Brumbeloe, Finis A.
- Burkitt, Benajah G.
- Butler, Milton C.
- Casello, John J.
- Castle, John A.
- Cecchini, Anthony J.
- Christian, Max A.
- Clifton, David S.
- Cogswell, Robert W.
- Connelly, Ben L.
- Coppom, John F.
- Crawford, William C.
- Crockett, George W. Jr.
- Crook, Charles D.
- DeWall, Hershel R.
- Edmunds, Robert E.
- Eisele, Roy
- Erickson, Roger W.
- Michaelis, Arthur D.
- Yarnall, Winfield L.
- Wolford, Roy V.
- Wirth, Gordon L.
- Mehlhoff, Arthur R.

- Farrar, John W.
- Fink, Marvin P. "Mike"
- Fisher, Dale M.
- Flickenger, Paul F.
- Foley, Norment
- Fontana, Bernard C.
- Fowler, Robert R.
- Fredericks, Jacob W.
- Fyler, Carl J.
- Geiger, James E.
- Glass, Henry F.
- Gravrock, Howard G.
- Griffin, Loyd D.
- Hahn, James T.
- Hallden, Robert H.
- Hallum, Bertrand C. Jr.
- Hardin, Thomas H. Jr.
- Hatch, Logan B.
- Heller, William C.
- Hobbs, Willard
- Holdcroft, Lloyd L.
- Hunsinger, Walter W.
- Johnston, Donald M.
- Jokerst, Leonard E.
- Jones, William E.
- Juns, Frank ,Jr.
- Kuykendall, Roger L.
- Kyle, George A.
- Lacker, Howard C.
- Lawlor, John C. Jr.
- Lester, Jack L.
- Long, John A.
- Luke, George W. Jr.
- Lyle, Lewis E.
- Lynch, Robert J.
- Mack, David W.
- Maker, Eugene L.
- McCormack, John E.
- McCutchan, Eugene R.
- McMillan, Murdock B. Jr.

- Middlemas, Arthur B.
- Miller, Edgar C.
- Morrin, John R.
- Mosel, Arnold P.
- Nafius, V. Harry
- O'Beirne, Nelson B.
- Osborn, William C.
- Palmer, Joseph F.
- Parker, John T.
- Parrott, John H.
- Railing, Charles F.
- Rapp, John W.
- Sapak, Aloysius I.
- Schulstad, Louis M.
- Scott, John
- Shields, Edward F. Jr.
- Shields, Emerson H.
- Skerpon, Melvin
- Smith, Samuel W.
- Spindler, Benjamin L.
- Stallings, George V. Jr.
- Stark, Donald D.
- Statton, Roy F.
- Stephan, Paul C.
- Stiver, Merrill M.
- St. Julien, John D.
- Stouse, Harold L.
- Tippet, Paul S.
- Thomas, Earl N.
- Underwood, George E.
- Vail, Robert F.
- Van Geyten, John J.
- Van Wie, John A.
- Vitale, Hector F.
- Vukovich, Emil J.
- Way, Arthur C.
- Weaver, Jack W.
- Welshon, Frank E. Jr.
- Williams, John T.
- Wilson, Fred F.

This is a list of the original pilots of the 360th Bombardment Squadron. (List courtesy of the 303rd Bomb Group.)

Pilots of the 427th BS

- Ackerman, Stewart S.
- Alderman, Melvin
- Ayers, Roger D.
- Barnes, Deane L.
- Barr, Thomas J.
- Barrat, Robert J.
- Beiser, Theodore R.
- Bliss, Robert P.
- Bohle, Howard J.
- Broussard, Edward J.
- Brown, Tracy D.
- Burch, Armand F.
- Callahan, Charles A.
- Caplinger, Auston O.
- Cassels, James C.
- Chuba, Francis B.
- Clark, Henry C.
- Cole, Lloyd R.
- Cook, Harry S.
- Cote, Addell A.
- Cureton, Peter F. Jr.
- Demian, Julius Carl
- Denison, William A.
- Donalson, David S.
- Drewry, James A.
- DuBose, Carl L. Jr.
- Duncan, Thomas A.
- Eckhart, Alan
- Eisenwinter, Philip D.
- Estes, Shirley E.
- Fisher, James H.
- Flanigan, Lloyd J.
- Fletcher, John E.
- Flick, Chester Eugene
- Flowers, Selwyn D.
- Fowler, James F
- Gano, Frederick
- Glasgow, Charles G.
- Goetz, William H.
- Grob, Emil E.
- Hamilton, Max B.
- Harrison, Emmittes S. Jr.
- Hayes, Ralph S.
- Healy, Richard F.
- Hullar, Robert
- James, Jacob C.
- Johnson, Charles E. Jr.
- Johnson, Charles E. Jr.
- Jones, Wilbur H.
- Kahler, Thomas F.
- Klint, Wilbur Bud
- Krohn, Robert W.
- LeFevre, William C.
- Lehmann, Elroy C. "Al"
- Ligino, Steve
- Lipe, Fort W.
- Lonski, Charlie J.
- Mars, Charles W.
- McClellan, George S.
- McGarry, John J.
- Melton, James H.
- Miller, Forrest E.
- Nemer, Alfred K.
- Ness, Howard C.
- Newton, George C.
- Newton, John A.
- O'Leary, James W.
- Peterson, William H.
- Pratt, James N.
- Reber, Ehle H.
- Reid, Clair P.
- Richardson, Thomas W.
- Robey, Harry A.
- Rolfson, Jack G.
- Rose, Jack W.
- Roy, Arnold K.
- Sabine, George E.
- Schlecht, Walter J.
- Sheets, Robert W.
- Shelhamer, David P.
- Shope, George W. Jr.
- Smith, Grafton N.
- Southworth, Billy B.
- Sterling, Jay R.
- Stockton, Donald E.
- Strickland, Alexander C.
- Sullivan, Francis X.
- Thomas, Blaine E.
- Turinsky, George
- Wardowski, Stanley
- Wertz, Robert W.
- Woddrop, Edward M.
- Wood, Vere A.

This is a list of the original pilots of the 427th Bombardment Squadron. (List courtesy of the 303rd Bomb Group.)

This is a certificate that was distributed to citizens of Massachusetts who fought in World War II to express the gratitude of the state for their efforts.

THE COMMONWEALTH OF
MASSACHUSETTS

IN RECOGNITION OF THE SERVICE OF

Kasmer Wegrzyn

IN THE ARMED FORCES OF THE
UNITED STATES OF AMERICA

PRESENTS THIS TESTIMONIAL
OF ESTEEM AND GRATITUDE FOR
FAITHFUL PERFORMANCE
OF DUTIES IN

WORLD WAR II

Maurice J. Tobin
GOVERNOR

W. H. Harrison
THE ADJUTANT GENERAL

This is the 303rd Bombardment Group's flag, bearing the group's slogan "Might in Flight." (Photograph courtesy of the 303rd Bomb Group.)

The Hell's Angels should be remembered as young men who sacrificed everything for their country and who made the best of it. Many of these men went home after the war to join or start families, run successful businesses, dedicate their lives to public service, or continue with the U.S. Army Air Force. Many of them did not make it home, but to all of them we say thank you. In this photograph, Sgt. Kasmer Wegrzyn (right) is shown sharing a "high five" with an unidentified member of the Hell's Angels.